How and why do animals adapt?

Bobbie Kalman

Crabtree Publishing Company
www.crabtreebooks.com

Dedicated by Bobbie and Peter
for Kyle Joseph Pinkerton,
who loves cars and tractors.
Vroom, vroom, Kyle!

Author and editor-in-chief
Bobbie Kalman

Publishing plan research and development
Reagan Miller

Editor
Kathy Middleton

Proofreader
Crystal Sikkens

Design
Bobbie Kalman
Katherine Berti
Samantha Crabtree (logo)

Photo research
Bobbie Kalman

Prepress technician
Samara Parent

Print and production coordinator
Margaret Amy Salter

Illustration
Barbara Bedell: page 18 (top)

Photographs
Thinkstock: page 12 (top); page 22 (bottom)
Wikimedia Commons: Fred Hsu: Matschies tree kangaroo
    at Bronx Zoo: page 7 (top right)
Cover and all other photographs by Shutterstock

Library and Archives Canada Cataloguing in Publication

Kalman, Bobbie, author
        How and why do animals adapt? / Bobbie Kalman.

(All about animals close-up)
Includes index.
Issued in print and electronic formats.
ISBN 978-0-7787-1463-7 (bound).--ISBN 978-0-7787-1471-2 (pbk.).--
ISBN 978-1-4271-7635-6 (pdf).--ISBN 978-1-4271-7629-5 (html)

        1. Animals--Adaptation--Juvenile literature. I. Title.

QL49.K3324 2015   j591.4   C2014-908180-4
                                                 C2014-908181-2

Library of Congress Cataloging-in-Publication Data

Kalman, Bobbie.
 How and why do animals adapt? / Bobbie Kalman.
    pages cm. -- (All about animals close-up)
 Includes index.
 ISBN 978-0-7787-1463-7 (reinforced library binding : alk. paper) --
 ISBN 978-0-7787-1471-2 (pbk. : alk. paper) --
 ISBN 978-1-4271-7635-6 (electronic pdf : alk. paper) --
 ISBN 978-1-4271-7629-5 (electronic html : alk. paper)
 1. Animals--Adaptation--Juvenile literature. I. Title.

QL49.K293183 2015
591.4--dc23
                                    2014046818

Crabtree Publishing Company

Printed in Canada/042015/BF20150203

www.crabtreebooks.com   1-800-387-7650

Published in Canada
Crabtree Publishing
616 Welland Ave.
St. Catharines, Ontario
L2M 5V6

Published in the United States
Crabtree Publishing
PMB 59051
350 Fifth Avenue, 59th Floor
New York, New York 10118

Published in the United Kingdom
Crabtree Publishing
Maritime House
Basin Road North, Hove
BN41 1WR

Published in Australia
Crabtree Publishing
3 Charles Street
Coburg North
VIC 3058

Contents

Why do animals adapt?

Sometimes when there are big changes in an animal's life, the animal has to change to stay alive. Changing to suit a new **habitat** is called adaptation. Animals adapt to find food, survive hot or cold temperatures, and escape danger. The animals that adapt easily are the ones that have the best chance of staying alive.

Most penguins live in icy cold areas, but yellow-eyed penguins make their nests in forests near ocean shores in New Zealand. They have adapted to living in a much warmer habitat.

Old and new adaptations

Many animal adaptations have happened over hundreds or even millions of years. Some happen more quickly. Adaptations can happen in the body or in the way an animal behaves.

This coywolf pup lives in a city park. Coywolves are part coyote and part wolf. Their bodies and ways of life have changed to survive living near people (see page 21).

The arctic fox lives in a very cold part of Earth, which is covered in ice and snow. It has thick white fur and tiny ears. Small ears keep heat inside the body of the fox.

What do you think?

How are the ears of the arctic fox different from the ears of the fennec fox on page 8? Why do you think the arctic fox is white in winter?

5

Changing how they move

Changing the ways they move has helped some animals get from place to place faster. Birds and bats made one of the biggest adaptations when their bodies changed so they could fly. Other animals have also adapted their ways of moving to suit new habitats or keep themselves safe.

*A dolphin is a **mammal**. Its flippers are made up of fingers under its skin. It uses its flippers to swim.*

fingers

Bats are the only mammals that fly. Many years ago, they were small animals that lived in trees. Their bodies changed so they could find more food. Their long fingers now support their wings.

flipper

Climbing trees

Most kangaroos hop along the ground, but one kind of kangaroo climbs trees and lives up in the branches. Tree kangaroos have adapted to living in trees because forests grew in their habitats, and they could find more food up in the trees.

tree kangaroo

claws

long front legs

short back legs

very long tail

kangaroo that hops

short tail

short front legs

long back legs

The bodies of tree kangaroos cause them to be clumsy on the ground but allow them to climb trees easily. Tree kangaroos have claws and pads on their feet for gripping tree bark, a long tail for balancing, and shorter back legs than the kangaroos that hop, shown left. Short back legs are better for climbing.

7

Adapting to deserts

Deserts are dry places with very little rain. Few plants grow in deserts because they are so dry, so animals that live there must adapt in order to find enough food and water to stay alive. Camels, for example, store fat in humps on their backs. The fat provides them with energy when they cannot find food or water. Some animals live in burrows, or holes, to stay out of the sun.

burrow

*The body of the fennec fox has adapted to its hot, dry desert home. Its long ears allow heat to escape from its body and to hear **prey** moving underground. The fox gets water from the food it eats. To hide from the hot sun, the fox spends most of its day in an underground burrow it has dug in the sand.*

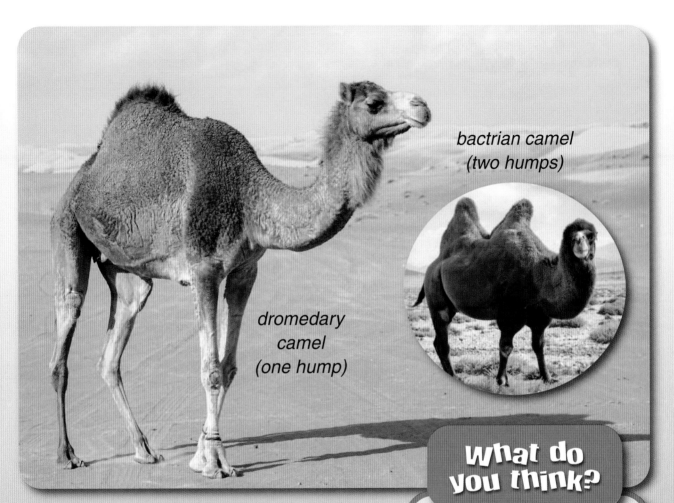

bactrian camel
(two humps)

dromedary
camel
(one hump)

Camels are suited to the desert habitats in which they live. They have one or two humps that are filled with fat. When they cannot find water for a long time, their body breaks down the fat into food energy. Camels have also adapted to keep water from leaving their bodies. They very rarely sweat.

What do you think?

The colors of the fennec fox and camel blend in with their sandy habitat. How does blending in keep these animals safe?

9

Winter adaptations

Some animals live in cold places for all or part of the year. Body adaptations and changes in behavior keep them warm in freezing-cold temperatures.

The snow leopard has adapted to winter in its rocky mountain home.

The leopard's thick fur keeps it warm. Its long tail helps it balance.

Its big chest helps it breathe the thin air high up on mountains.

The leopard's big paws help it walk and climb in snow.

A bear sleeps during much of winter. It wakes up on warmer days to stretch or snack on stored food.

what do you think?

How do you keep your body warm in winter? How are your winter adaptations the same or different from those of animals?

Leaving their habitats

Canada geese

Many animals migrate, or move to other habitats, to escape cold weather, find food and water, or have babies. Many kinds of birds, such as Canada geese and arctic terns, migrate to warmer places for the winter.

Arctic terns migrate the farthest. They fly from the North Pole to the South Pole and back again.

Humpback whales migrate from cold oceans to warm oceans to give birth to their calves, or babies.

The mothers and calves swim back to cold oceans when the calves have put on enough fat to keep them warm.

Some animals lose their homes because people cut down forests or build farms where the animals once lived. This baby elephant has gone under an electric fence built by a farmer, but its mother is not able to fit under it.

What do you think?

Why do people travel in winter? Why do they move from one home to another? How many times have you moved? Why did you move?

Living in groups

One of the most important adaptations animals have made is living in groups. Animals that belong to families or **communities** can help one another find food and keep safe. Examples of animal groups are monkey troops, lion prides, dolphin pods, and meerkat mobs.

*Meerkats live in mobs of 20 to 30 members. They live in large underground homes. Groups of meerkats guard their homes and watch for **predators** while others look for food. Working together helps keep these animals alive.*

grooming

(above) Groups of Japanese macaque monkeys, also called snow monkeys, keep warm in pools that are heated by nature. (right) The monkeys groom, or keep one another clean, as a way of being friendly.

What do you think?

Name five groups that are important in your community. How does each group give you the things you need to keep safe and be happy?

15

The great pretenders

Some animals have developed coloring or patterns on their bodies that help them blend in with their habitats. This is called camouflage. Camouflage helps hide them from predators or prey. Many animals also use mimicry. Mimicry makes animals look like plants or other animals, making it hard to tell what or where they are.

Did you guess that this scary looking animal is a small insect called a praying mantis?

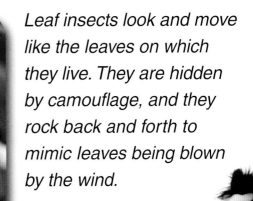

Leaf insects look and move like the leaves on which they live. They are hidden by camouflage, and they rock back and forth to mimic leaves being blown by the wind.

Praying mantises often mimic flowers, leaves, and branches. This mantis is called a spiny flower mantis.

What do you think?

Name five ways you mimic other people or things. How, when, and why do you do it? What costumes have you worn? When do you wear them?

New kinds of animals

The bodies of some animals have changed so much that it is hard to believe that they are part of the animal groups to which they belong. Mudskippers, tree shrews, and aye-ayes are just a few examples.

Mudskippers are fish that can live on land as well as in water. They can walk, skip, leap, dig, and swim. They can even climb trees! These fish can breathe through their mouths and skin.

Unlike other lemurs, aye-ayes have developed teeth like **rodents** for chewing and long middle fingers for pulling bugs out of trees. Their long toes also allow them to hang from branches.

long front teeth

long fingers

long toes

Tree shrews look like squirrels but have bigger brains. Inside their bodies, they are more like **primates** such as monkeys.

Adapting to city life

Many animals must live in cities when cities take up the land that was once their habitats. Some animals adapt easily to city life and live longer because they can find more food there. City animals include squirrels, foxes, coyotes, coywolves, raccoons, opossums, and skunks.

*Omnivores are animals that eat both plants and other animals. They have a much better chance of surviving in cities than **herbivores** or **carnivores**. Many omnivores eat almost anything they find. This raccoon omnivore is eating a pet cat's food.*

Squirrels find the food they need in trees and in people's back yards.

Red foxes are omnivores that can find plenty of animals to hunt in cities, such as squirrels, rats, and mice. They also eat plant foods.

Skunks often live under people's decks or garages. They dig up grass looking for **grubs** to eat.

The coywolf is part coyote and part wolf. It is bigger than a coyote and lives much longer than both animals. The coywolf is one of the most adaptable animals on Earth. It lives in many cities, including Toronto and New York City.

How do you adapt?

Compare and contrast your adaptations to those of the animals in this book. Write stories about how you have adapted to changes in your life. Use some of the ideas in the box on the right.

- *moving to a new home*
- *summer and winter changes*
- *learning to swim or snowboard*
- *being part of different groups*
- *finding new friends*
- *speaking a new language*
- *learning new skills*
- *changing your thinking*

Learning more

Books

Kalman, Bobbie and Niki Walker. *How do animals adapt?* (The Science of Living Things). Crabtree Publishing Company, 2000.

Kalman, Bobbie. *An Animal Community* (My World). Crabtree Publishing Company, 2010.

Kalman, Bobbie. *What are Nature's Copycats?* (Big Science Ideas). Crabtree Publishing Company, 2012.

Kalman, Bobbie. *Baby Animals in Cities* (The Habitats of Baby Animals). Crabtree Publishing Company, 2013.

Rose, Elizabeth. *Animal Adaptations for Survival* (Life Science Library). Powerkids Press, 2006.

Murphy, Julie. *Desert Animal Adaptations* (Amazing Animal Adaptations). Capstone Press, 2011.

Websites

Interactive sites for education: Animal Adaptations
http://interactivesites.weebly.com/animal-adaptations.html

Youtube: Animal Adaptations
www.youtube.com/watch?v=fRX2JtKFUzk

Youtube: How Animals Adapt (Animal Atlas)
www.youtube.com/watch?v=z4xFDjy3uT8

Words to know

carnivore (KAHR-nuh-vawr) noun
An animal that eats mainly meat
community (KUH-myoo-ni-tee) noun
A place or the group of living things
that shares that place
grub (gruhb) noun The wormlike young
of certain beetles or other insects
habitat (HAB-i-tat) noun The natural
place where a plant or animal lives
herbivore (HUR-buh-vawr) noun
An animal that eats mainly plants

mammal (MAM-uh-l) noun A warm-blooded
animal that gives birth to live young
predator (PRED-uh-ter) noun An animal
that hunts and eats other animals
prey (prey) noun An animal that is hunted
and eaten by another animal
primate (PRAHY-meyt) noun A very
smart mammal, such as a monkey or ape
rodent (ROHD-nt) noun A mammal with
front teeth that never stop growing

A noun is a person, place, or thing.

Index

24